A Poetry Collection

Thirty,

Flirty,

and

Thriving

Published by LB Publishing, LLC

Original edition ISBN: 979-8-9918718-2-2

A Poetry Collection – Thirty, flirty, and trying. Copyright © 2025 by Lanna Brasure

All rights reserved.

A collection of poetry
written by Lanna Brasure

I am radically scared that I will lose all of my memories one day. So this is my way of holding onto them and letting them live, let all the versions of myself live.

A *C*ollection of poems I wrote shortly before and shortly after turning thirty.

In between these pages, you will find emotional expression for the passing of my mom, the losing of myself, going through divorce, living on my own for the first time in my entire life, building myself, navigating my individual life's purpose, trying to make sense of things, and all of the love I give so freely.

We all long to connect and resonate with others.

And, to feel something.

I release these words into the world in hopes of that –

that you feel something.

♥

I'm not sure if I've ever been in love.
Or if I've just wanted to capture people.
Obtain them for a moment.
The way some have wanted to obtain me.
The way a child captures a butterfly in a glass jar and calls it beautiful.
Only to suffocate it completely.

I think I've confused people into thinking I'm in love with them.

And in turn I've confused myself.

By being kind.

Lending a helping hand.

Lending an open ear.

I think being nice has been interpreted and digested as "this woman is into me"

And I think in turn, it's confused me.

Led me down the path of love even if I wasn't in love.

Without really knowing whether or not I am.

They think I love them so I shall.

Why would I help if I didn't?

Or is it just that I want to fix people so much?

Help them to mend the parts of them they can't mend on their own.

Help them to see the beauty that they may not see.

Let me help.

Please let me help.

But, do I just help them cross the street?

Or, do I wrap myself up in this person's life, this person's being, and never let go.

Until the next person has to be helped.

It should be normal to go off and find ourselves if and when we need to.

You shouldn't want a person to be half of themselves.

We are allowed to be and feel liberated.

I have a wedding dress, a dinosaur, and some skeletons in my closet.

I found my courage once before but I think I've already lost it.

A testament of wisdom but signed with such despair.

Forever knowing that my here will always be better than any there.

Clouded judgement disguised as movement,

I said I'd never do it. But the only way to get over it is to go right fucking through it.

Missing my passions and having to prove it.

Getting graded because it was school and

Having to work hard to make things work because you were determined to do it.

I have some unused skeletons in my closet, I hate them.

Just like emotions they'll all be donated.

Here I am now.

Feelings are gated.

I've loved too many of you.

What if there isn't a set, specific reason for why our heart doesn't want to be with a person?

What if, we long for someone, and we desire a connection with them, but our heart can't fully grasp onto them?

What if our mind so badly wants it that it tries to convince our souls it's meant to be?

Only to find our bodies physically pulling us away.

We can't figure out why we don't want to be with this person.

It's usually so obvious.

They have bad breath, commitment issues, they're not close with their family, they're too close with their family, they don't have any goals, they work too much, they don't have a job, they have different views, different opinions, your morals don't align, your core values don't align, they suck at driving.

Sometimes it's so easy to see.

So when we can't put our literal finger on it because it's not entirely tangible we start to doubt that it's not meant to be, we fight our soul, and our brain tries to make it work.

Sometimes we can't put our finger on it.

Sometimes we're still drawn to a person and want the connection.

But something feels off.

We can't figure out what it is because it's not in our list of flaws we've collected throughout the years of failed relationships and missed opportunities.

But sometimes, everything *is* perfect.

The connection *is* there.

The compatibility.

Chemistry.

Morals, opinions, safety, goals, and driving records all intact.

Those are the real tests in life.

When it *is* all perfect and you know you still have to walk away.

When you don't let the perfection distract you.

It's not that you need better, a better to the perfect.

You just know not everything is meant for you.

And no matter how ripe, how delicious, how juicy, something may be...

Not everybody likes peaches.

I'll never be in this place again.
In this moment of my life.
I'll never be this version of myself ever again.
I'll never have this apartment again.
I may never be in this location again.
With this energy again.
I'll never be this young again.
I'll never be any of this ever again.
So I need to live my life out exactly as the way I am in this moment in time.
I need to embrace everything as it is right now.
Because it will never be the same ever again.

Life is what you make it.

I used to think that meant perspective.

Life is what you make it out to be.

Now I believe life is what you make it.

What you make it to be.

What you build to become your life.

Even if it's little, even if it's small.

This is my sanctuary, between these 4 walls.

Sometimes the breeze reminds me that things are possible.
I'm not sure what it is.
But I can feel it when it touches my skin.
My hair.
My soul.

Was it my mom that saved me?

My grams?

Was it a random ghost who thought I should have a chance?

Who were you?

Was it the universe as a whole?

Or nothing at all?

Was it just a random moment I looked up at the time and it was screaming at me, "don't do it!"

I don't know how to add it all up.

Or if it needs to be added up at all.

Maybe it was just myself.

Convincing myself it was a greater being telling me I am worthy of staying.

Maybe I am that greater being.

I am worthy of staying.

I am worthy of telling myself I can stay.

Should stay.

Will stay.

Maybe I am what saved me and I am still so in awe that I could have that power, that will power, to save my own self knowing damn well what is going on in my damn head.

To be saved by others, to be saved by ourselves, to be saved at all.

I'm not sure if it matters anymore who "you" were exactly.

Maybe we are all the same person, spirit, soul, being, exploded into multiple peoples running around the world trying to find themselves and save each other.

If we connect more with others, maybe we find ourselves more.

Maybe we become cosmically charged and for a moment can tell "I am this person, I see myself in this person, and them in me. We are one. We are all one."

And I hope that we can all save each other and ourselves by saving ourselves and each other.

You can't always wait until
someone else believes in you
and tells you you're great.
Sometimes you just have to feel it
in yourself and do.
And if you can't feel it yet,
then just do.

I hardly ever bake anymore,

My house is always clean.

And without a doubt, Out of everyone,

Caidy will know what that means.

If you were the person you wanted to be tomorrow, what would you look like today?

Would you be standing outside of a tall building in a suit holding a briefcase?

Would you look super successful with your million-dollar bills?

Would you be at the top of a mountain gaining all the thrills?

What would you look like today

if you were what you wanted to be tomorrow?

Would it really be so different?

What a pill to swallow.

Wouldn't you look the same?

Oh, what a sudden change!

If the person we wanted to be,

were only a day away.

When you romanticize your life, you romanticize the good and the bad. You sit with your emotions a little longer. Feel them completely. Let them flow through you. Acknowledge them. Acknowledge this moment. Don't dismiss the happiness, or the pain for that matter. Embrace the feeling of *feeling*. Take it in. And then move forward. Into more blissful states of being. And feeling.

I've always wondered what my purpose is.

Chef.

Guidance counselor.

Fashion designer.

Lawyer.

Psychologist.

Business owner.

Mentor.

Teacher.

Software Engineer.

Coach.

Leader.

I realized my purpose is not any title I could ever hold.

My purpose is who I am.

My purpose is the kindness I spread.

My purpose is me showing up as my most authentic self so you feel like you can too.

I spread vulnerability and rawness.

The kind of connection you feel you knew ages ago when we just met.

My purpose is to be a glimpse of beauty in this wild world.

To be gentle and humorous.

Humble and considerate.

Friendly banter and honest discussions.

My purpose can last a lifetime or a few seconds depending on our meet cute.

But, there is still purpose no matter how long.

Whether you're a dear friend who can call me when sad and talk for hours,

Or someone passing by who sees me open the door for someone that inspires them to later open the door for someone else.

My purpose is not to create a successful business, or to make millions, or to become famous.

My purpose is to be me.

To show up as me every time.

I've been searching for my purpose for so long.

And I always thought it would be so hard to fulfill it once I figured out what it was.

But, it turns out, it's the easiest thing.

Because all I have to do is be me.

And spread love.

That is my purpose.

To love.

Every one.

And every thing.

Equally.

So that they may spread that same love.

To every one.

And every thing.

And maybe with one person and one thing at a time,

I can change the world.

Decision Paralysis

You're going to sit here and you're going to pout.

Until it's dark and until it's gloomy.

Until it's not your decision to make anymore.

You're going to stay stuck in frustrated pout until you surrender that there is no decision.

Your anxiety has won again.

Maybe you will go for the walk tomorrow.

What the fuck even happened?

We were so happy at one point..

I was coming over every night, getting ready on my way to see you.

Making out as soon as we saw each other. We *were* passionate, weren't we?

What the fuck happened?

Did we want it too bad?

So bad?

That bad?!

I can't get over your laugh lines by your eyes.

It's a reason I've stayed.

I love making you happy.

Making you smile.

Is there more to that?

Why am I leaving?

The coldest winter for me,

Is coming up..

I hate hurting you. I never wanted this.

But, did I want any of this?

The marriage? The companionship? The relationship?

Why would I do this to a person?

Why am I changing?

So drastically.

Am I a monster?

I don't know if I can control this.

But do I even want to?

We were the perfect couple.

Weren't we?

What the fuck even happened?

I wish I could sift through this like the flour I use for my cakes.

Effortlessly and with minimal anxiety is preferred.

It doesn't feel right.

But that doesn't feel right either.

Where did we go wrong?

Where did I go wrong?

What the fuck even happened?!

Maybe that's why I don't share much of what I write.
Because it's about you.
And you.
And you.
And you, and you, and you.
And what I did to you.
What you did to me.
What we did to each other.
How it felt.
How it all felt.
The way you looked at me.
For how long you looked at me.
The way we were.
The way things were.
The way it all was.
It's about you.
And I can't be writing about you while you watch me.

What am I to do?

Just spend my days with you?

Just lay around, and putz around.

Just spend all day with you?

What am I to do?

Just live my days in you?

Consumed and doomed

and laced with you.

Just live by dazed induced?

What am I to do?

Just live unlikely, too?

a petite four,

a lonely door,

I missed it all like you.

So fuck you and you too.

I'll live for just me too.

and can you score but maybe more

anywhere else you choose.

Thank you to cookie brownies.

Only upside down frownies.

To not giving up and not giving in

And rolling with the pouncing.

You are not perfect

It'll all be ok

Everything is coming

Just not right away.

This storm too shall pass

And a victory awaits

Speak unto the universe

Create your own fate.

Reflections of candles

The city lights dim

Imagining the wrong

You would undo to him.

Timid and sheltered

Unleashed from within

Frightened by courage

Discouraged by sin.

If money were no object, how would you spend your time?

What would you do with your life?

Me?

I'd travel the world.

See all there is to see.

All of the beauty and even the grimy.

I'd spend time with loved ones as if we didn't have anywhere to rush to.

I'd take every day off to explore internally and externally.

I'd go to Paris and Italy to take cooking classes and learn how to make my own clothes.

I'd learn to talk like others and mess up the words and never forget who I am.

I'd stop striving for perfection and worry less about status.

The food I would eat.

The places I would go.

If money were no object, I'd follow my passions harder and longer.

Stronger and wiser.

I'd fill myself up to the brim with possibilities of all the things I so long to do.

So, if money were no object, what would you do?

If we stopped letting an almost weightless piece of man-made paper get in between you and your soul's desires.

A soul is more tangible to the human spirit than a dollar will ever be.

For I have touched souls that I have never let go of.

Yet every dollar has left my fingertips in the midst of a moment.

The gold standard of the heart is hope.

And we keep beating to see the future that we seek.

To go skydiving in New Zealand.

Hiking in every nook and cranny and park I can find.

To see architecture that only the brilliant minds saw in their head before they made it come to life in the big sky.

To learn from others.

To let others consume me.

Let it all consume me.

My experiences.

The ones I paid for and the ones I did not.

I want to live and I don't want to pay for all of the beauty.

My currency is curiosity.

I have enough to spread.

So what would you do if money were no object instead?

Go out on a limb, fuck it plant a whole tree

Out of your comfort zone, starting to see

If you believe in yourself and manage your health

You'll become who you're becoming to be.

Count your blessings like 1, 2, 3

Imaginary but real as can be

Manifestation and delayed gratification

Tied together by consistency.

An everlasting moment,

But those too shall pass,

Out of all the moments we experience today,

Some may be our last.

The last time we visit a coffee shop,

That decides to close their doors,

While they move on to continue their journey,

And you continue yours.

A restaurant down the street,

that didn't make it from that year,

Walking to it every week,

Taking away recipe ideas.

Places that made you feel calm,

That no longer exist,

Walking into them for the last time,

Not knowing they'll soon be missed.

Talks at the old salon,

Leaving a job without a hug,

Keeping connections in my cupboard,

represented by coffee mugs.

How do we really know,

When it'll be our last,

Time to experience something?

Our one final chance.

Putting apron capes on with Mandy,

and dances on the line,

Singing with other cooks,

and playing speed to pass the time.

The last time I used Doug's paring knife,

The last time I heard Scotty's voice,

The last time I gave her two hugs,

Before she made a delicate choice.

Playing house before a nap,

Playing office and painting nails,

Make the best of every moment,

And save all of your voicemails.

Chipotle chicken paninis,

A latte flight I didn't try,

Endless Sunday brunch,

Even the little things pass us by.

Charlie and Mac before they left,

Tiny crowded apartments,

Braiding every strand in our first house,

To only parallel parking.

Calls from my mom,

My ex-husband before I changed,

My grams' backyard,

Frankenmuth for 8.

Familiar places before the remodel,

The school haus and arcade,

One of my biggest regrets will be

Showing up to your last thanksgiving late.

There isn't always a sign up,

We won't always know,

That's why it's important to get up and get out,

And to make it before they close.

So overdo it when you have to,

Embrace the moment while you have it,

Frequent every person and place you love,

Take the full advantage.

Some people miss the Joe,

Or friends who live over seas,

I miss all the people and places

Who ever made me feel like me.

An engineer who answered my questions,

A friend who made me feel seen,

The last time I saw any lovers,

Who I used to love and they used to love me.

And sometimes we hold back,

The love we want to show,

But it's important to give your love to others

Because they may not always know.

And don't not go to the party,

Only leave when you're ready to leave,

You don't want your life to be a series

of missed opportunities.

Be grateful for the little mess in your little one-bedroom apartment.

Because messes in mansions are much worse.

I've been drowning myself in thoughts of why we shouldn't be together.

Of why it didn't work out.

Of why I couldn't give myself to you fully.

I'm sorry I was ashamed.

I was never ashamed of you.

I was ashamed of me and the decisions that I made to take me to that point.

Whether or not we were great, I still wish I never went through that period in my life and hurt the people I hurt.

I learned that, I couldn't give myself to you fully because I wasn't fully available.

I was left with nothing. And I didn't realize the new trauma I was building up for me to deal with later.

None of that matters for the purpose of this other than that is why I couldn't love you fully.

Even though on some days it felt like it.

You showed me the most playful love I have ever known.

I love you so fucking much.

And I am so fucking sorry.

And I wish you absolutely nothing but the absolute best.

I think I confuse love and excitement.
I need to get better with my words.
I need to get better with my emotions.

I wish I had never sought it.

It never seemed right, I just bought it.

And then after I had it, I didn't even wear it.

And now it's in the back of my closet.

I thought I could push it back; Be forgotten

Taking up space in my head, almost lost it.

But it's been pushing back, screaming what I once had

Telling me lies as if it's something I wanted.

On some days I feel like it's taunting,

Fuck that it's mostly just daunting

For the day that it's out in someone else's house

The doubt is a cloud; it's a haunting.

I'll put something else there, a coat or some boxes.

Keep the tags, I'm cutting my losses.

From what I once was, I swear I was in love,

Next time I'll read all of the clauses.

The mental debt from altering what I started,

The back and the forth was just constant,

Being in my head, a truth unsaid,

Losing myself in the process is how I responded.

Laced with distress, turned the pain into a sonnet,

I promise he will never be forgotten.

But I must release the burden of all of the hurt and

Remove my past from the back of my closet.

Self-doubt makes me feel like I'm not living my life to the fullest or like I'm not living up to my potential. It prevents me from doing things I love. I want to do things I love.

There are certain things in life in which we long for that we have no control over.

Who we love.

Where our soul feels it needs to travel to.

Leaving a job.

Leaving a loved one.

The sense of being alone.

The need to be surrounded.

There are certain things in this life in which we cannot control.

We do not possess the ability to overcome the strongest emotions of where our invisible soul will take our entirely tangible being.

For those moments, are the easiest decisions I've ever made.

Some the hardest, when my brain didn't understand where my heart was taking my body.

But I understand now.

To understand why we were taken there isn't always important though.

To embrace our time in each place is what we focus on.

And that is what I long for.

To focus on each, single, separate, individual moment, as if each one were the only one I would ever live in.

Cross my t's and dot my I's
Sometimes I'm in love
Looking back and I'll tell you
I thought he was the one

Growing now with hindsight eyes
Bending time I'll tell you truth
I think that I've loved everyone
From a different point of view

I'm just a girl, living in Detroit,

Trying to take it day by day.

I wished for what I wanted

And was surprised when I got it,

But, you know what they say.

Careless in envy

All rattled, all shook

I let the darkness creep in again

Until I reach out

I call to the clouds,

Begging for it to end.

A dire compassion,

How did I let that all happen.

Maybe one day it will stop.

Having the courage and discipline

To be intentional about my own thoughts.

Sticky and wet,

The discomfort to grow,

One day I will be me.

But I open my eyes.

I open my mind.

I am becoming who I'm becoming to be.

A note to myself,

A note to who needs it,

A note to anyone who feels when they read it.

I said it before, and I did mean it.

We are going to be ok.

I think a way to realize or find our purpose is to do the things that call us

To do the things that make us feel alive and in approval of our soul

Sometimes we see something that someone else is doing, and we think, "I can do that", or, "I can do that better"

That's not your calling.

That's your ego.

Just because we can do something doesn't always mean it's our calling.

Find what calls you.

If you're having trouble making art, just romanticize everything.

"She was walking to get breakfast and she decided to stop at the garden and smell the roses."

No.

"She was walking to her most favorite breakfast place and she had planned to stop at the garden every single time she had passed it. She had not only planned on smelling the roses, but she would frolic through each line of flowers to see what new had bloomed. She didn't just smell the roses, she basked in the feeling of possibility this garden made her feel. She stopped to smell the hyacinths, the daffodils, the lavender, the snap dragons, even if it didn't have a scent she was going to put her face in it. She would stop at the garden because it was not only a reminder of how beautiful growth is, but it reminded her of her mom. Her mom and her love of flowers, the garden she had, and her grams' gardens. And she thought maybe, just maybe every time she saw a butterfly that it was her mom coming to visit. She would leave the garden refreshed feeling anew, headed to her most favorite breakfast place in the city where she had learned everyone's name and they had learned hers. Where they had all learned each other's stories and parts of each other's lives. And she thought to herself, how anyone could ever feel alone in such a beautiful life."

A million questions.

A million questions I have for you,
Sitting inside my head.
But you're not here for me to ask them to,
So I'll write them out instead.

As I ponder them,
And sift through them all,
I wonder...
Would you be able to answer them all?

How do you feel about change,
and the struggles from within?
Am I alone when I feel this?
Or is it all kith and kin?

Did you hate your jobs?
How did you hang?
You made it through so much,
Sometimes I don't think I can.

Did you have close friends,
Who knew all of your secrets?
Sharing your deepest thoughts,
Hoping that they'd keep it?

Did you ever feel judged?
Or like you could be replaced?
Were there hard fears in your life,
You wished you never faced?

Was there a one,
Who got away?
Who you hoped you could tell
Your three girls about some day?

Did you love dad?
And was it true?
Were you happy?
Did you ever feel like you?

Are you proud,
Of us three girls?
Did we enhance your life,
Or damper your world?

Were we too much?
Did we take you away,
From pursuing your dreams,
And finding your way?

Are you proud of me?
Did I do well?
Are you mad at me,
For how things went?

Do you think that black holes
Are portals to other dimensions?
Do you think the time we have is enough?
Or can it be bended?

Can hearts be full,
After being mended?
And if you ever had an enemy,
Could they later be friended?

How did you navigate life,
With all the pain in the world?
How did you appear so strong,
In front of your three girls?

Did you enjoy your life?
Were you proud of you?
What would you do over again
If you really had to?

Would you experience,
Some things twice?
Would you skip past a memory,
That you didn't like?

What was your most favorite part,
Of this crazy life?
Was it being a mom?
Was it being a wife?

Was it being wild and free?
As I knew you to be.
Was it to think out of the box,
And just let it be?

I ponder them,
And they sift through my brain,
Like flour from cookies,
That we used to make.

Would you be proud of me?
About the things I have done?
Would you smile with grace,
At who I've become?

One million questions,
And I'd ask them all.
While we sit at the kitchen table
Ignoring every call.

What kind of woman were you,
Outside of mother and wife?
What were your aspirations?
What did you want out of life?

Were you in your own head?
Did you have confidence too?
I'm beating myself up trying to
Figure out what I got from you.

So many questions,
Floating in mid air,
To never be answered,
To never be shared.

But what does it matter
And why should I care?
I want to know where I come from!
And if my thoughts aren't that rare.

But I can't and I won't,
But I wish that I could have.
I wish I never hung up the phone earlier,
Than this version of me would have.

Please, stop..
No more questions.
All this sifting through my thoughts,
Is giving me depression.

But I consider it a lesson,
Advice to any friend,
Please don't hold all questions,
until the very end.

But one last thought,
I know it to be true.
As life goes on,
I'm learning more about you.

I've asked the universe these questions,
Sometimes slow in response,
But I'm filling in the gaps,
Like we once talked about.

You are here in particles,
I believe it to be mystical,
That I will get my answers
Even if not physical.

And the sadness is still there,
That will never part,
I think about it every day,
Especially in March.

But just as seasons change,
Emotions rearrange,
Feeling every feeling,
In every single stage.

I miss you and I love you,
And I think every butterfly has become you.
All these unasked questions,
But I really just want to hug you.

But I will let these questions rest in peace,
For my aching mind I put at ease,
Take the pain and let it release,
I wish I could have known you more.

bar seats

The nightly bar chair dance

the chairs go up

up they stay

until they are brought back down at the social hour

who will sit in them?

Will there be love shared between the seats?

Fights?

Stimulating conversations

Flirting between lovers across the way

laughter

joy

fear

quirkiness

what will there be

I could be one of them

We would just listen to music, make out, smoke weed, and do pole in my living room while we fell in love ~~with it all and each other.~~

It was all art.

I think of leaving next year

and I think of all the people and places I've frequented

I think about how I'll miss seeing their faces and feeling their presence

I think about the connections I made here

I don't have much holding me here

But it wouldn't be a home without the kind faces I see on a daily basis

Some I don't even know their names

But I do know it wouldn't be a home without the Caidys.

Without the Megans and the Jakes.

Without the Robs and the Einos at my favorite restaurant.

Or the Kens and the Nicoles at my favorite breakfast spot.

The Artys and the Amandas at the coffee shop I probably spend way too much money at.

The kind souls I got to bump into in the city just wandering about in a small big city.

The Ramseys and the Megans and the Danielles and the Melissas.

The Andrews and the Matts and the Brandens and the Debs.

The guy who for the last five years has asked me if I like hip hop.

The new people I meet on a moment's notice.

The McKaylas who taught me to laugh about it, because if we don't laugh about it we're going to cry about it.

The Elmuses who taught me that we are meant to share our knowledge and experiences with others, and that we are all creative and can find happiness if we choose it.

The self-proclaimed prophet Marcel.

The people who watch me draw sitting at a bar drinking lemonade and tell me I've made more progress than I think.

I am in love with the strangers who become a part of my soul.

I'll be back soon.

But man, will I miss it all.

Manifestation is about having a conversation with the universe that only you and it can hear, and it is put in motion when you are in the right vibrational frequency in which the universe knows you want, are ready, and deserving of this thing.

And I think, if you show grace during your waiting period, in the waiting room of fulfillment, I think the universe will give you exactly what you asked for.

I have this very strange
feeling within my soul
that I may be ready
for love again.

May be ready to live inside of the world I build with another human.

A world far better than the one around me.

A brighter one.

Full of more life and more love than the one I'm currently living in

I have this very strange feeling inside of my being that I may be ready to give love again.

I may be ready to shower a person with all of my energy and lovable feelings.

I'm beginning to understand the divine timing of things.
That we're not supposed to get everything that we want all at
once.
There's a trickling to our desires and we have to be patient as
our life fills up with them.
We must have grace during our waiting period.
There's a gratitude this instills in us.
A humbleness.
A reflection period when we realize we didn't even want it all.
As we learn our desires change.
Our patience.
Our levels of grace.
Divine timing is for us.
We need to embrace it.
Trust it.
Be guided by it.
And, be ok with not being guided at all.
Oh, divine timing.
I've been waiting for you.
And I know you will always be there.
At the right time.
When I need you.
Or perhaps not at all.
Because that is divine timing.
We may not always know why.
But the beauty is in not knowing and following the unknown.
To embrace all that is not yet.
That is, divine.

I think if I knew where the souls went,
I would feel better about the closing of someone's life.

my calling is caring

my calling is intimacy with everyone on every level

my calling is connection

compassion

chemistry

curiosity

my calling is sharing my experiences so you feel more connected
and less alone

my calling is to be a light for others

hope

possibility

my calling is me

to give myself to others

so they may feel joy in my presence

A lot of my healing knowledge and support has come from strangers on the internet.

Following people who are knowledgeable and have personal experience in an area of my life I want to be better in.

Most of these people have opened up more than those close to me outside of the virtual world.

That vulnerable sharing is what helps some of us heal.

To feel less alone.

To help us navigate where we are in life.

To relate.

To resonate.

To feel connected.

Isn't it wild that some of us feel more connected to strangers than we do our actual friends?

That we can learn more from people not as close to us.

I think we're all afraid.

That someone might find out we're not done growing yet.

That we're not fully bloomed.

Afraid someone may see we still make mistakes.

But we're never done growing.

We're never done making mistakes.

We're never really done learning.

It is impossible to achieve perfection even if we never died.

Maybe it's just the ego that needs to die.

So we can share more.

Share our stories more.

Our tales of healing.

Our experiences.

Our triumphs.

What we hate.

What we love.

Why we're weird and why that makes us wildly lovable.

What is it that prevents us from sharing more in hopes to heal each other?

Would it not heal you to share something that makes you feel alone only to find out other people feel the same?

What will we miss out on by not sharing more of ourselves with each other?

Not everything needs to be captured.

Some things are just meant to be experienced

To be felt.

With nothing to remain of it but the way it made us feel.

A memory that will fade.

The older I get, the more I understand my parents and others in my life.
Why they are the way they are or why they reacted a certain way in a memory I replay in my head.
As I sit in this coffee shop, I hear the song "I just called to say I love you"

I remember my mom had a teacup figurine that would play this song when you pushed the button on the bottom.
I can't remember exactly if she got that from her mom, or if we got it for my mom after her mom passed.
Either way, it very much reminded her of her mom.

One day, without thinking anything of it, I pushed the button. She tried to stop me.
I didn't understand.
She seemed sad that the song was playing.
I didn't understand why that would bother her.
She loved her mom.
So much.

Now that I'm older and have gone through my own grieving process of my own mother, I understand.
I understand so much now.

That song triggered her.
She didn't want to experience those emotions or the flood of
memories that that song would trigger.

I feel bad now.
I feel bad for not understanding.
Which is silly, I didn't know any better and I was so young.

But, it does make me second guess someone's emotional
state before I think about pressing any buttons.

We are all on journeys.

Sometimes it will happen in the shower when you're shaving your legs.
Sometimes when you're trying to make a form of potato pancakes.
It could be in a new friend you meet.
Or someone you were finally able to let go of.
The point is it doesn't happen overnight.
It doesn't happen after the first therapy session.
Or second.
Or usually any of them.
It doesn't happen from buying the self-help books.
Buying the journals.
Making the lists.
But when you put in the work you will get epiphanies and glimpses of light, glimpses of clarity.
The accumulation of everything you've done will start to show.
Will start to feel.
The daily journal entries.
The therapy visits.
The books read.
The podcasts listened to.
The research and data consumed, experiments ran, data collected, reflection, awareness, action, inspiration, continuous movement and growth..
You will start to feel it.
One more piece of the healing puzzle is complete.

Your rawness is your home.
Being all that you are.
All that you want to be or don't want to be.
Not your authenticity; it's more than that.
Under the skin, within you, a place we have no name for.
Rawness?
Not even your heart is your home as it has a tendency to play
tricks on us.
Not our soul for we need rawness to reveal it.
It feels intimate.
Naked.
Not sexual.
Not sensual.
Deepening.
Not awakening.
Peacening.
A resonation.
An understanding.
A bond.
A commitment.
To helping each other feel less lone.
Who do you let come into your home?

I always wondered why artists were so messy.

It seemed like they always lived in a mess of chaos and they were never bothered by it.

As someone who has always been organized, I couldn't see myself living that way.

Most of the time, I need a clean, tidy, organized environment in order to create anything.

Otherwise my mind is a mess.

It's cluttered...like the space I'm in.

Cleaning my apartment clears my mind and allows me to create better.

Until the cleaning begins to take up more space than the creating.

When motivation is being used for straightening up instead of pursuing your dreams.

I notice as time goes on, the more art I create, the messier my apartment is.

The more pages I write, the less I care about the dishes or wiping down the counters.

The less diligent I am to do the task I've been putting off for 2 weeks.

The more progress I make on my passion projects, the less likely I am to straighten my hair.

The less motivation I have to care about my outfit.

I've noticed, with more ideas comes more procrastination, but also comes with less vacuuming.

The brainstorming sessions with the other creators in my head come before putting laundry away.

And my attempts at illustrating comes before grocery shopping.

I've realized, I can live in this chaos, as long as art is the result.

I can tidy up on a Tuesday afternoon,

But when that inspiration and motivation comes to write or draw or dance or sing or create at whatever day and time it chooses...

When that feeling sets in...

Even when I need to go get my mail and packages I've left downstairs for 3 weeks...

I will choose art every time.

The only thing I let myself fixate on now is to be as comfortable in that seat as I can be to let the words flow through and out of me.

I've attracted more people with me being myself than me being closed off.
I've resonated with more people now than when I didn't reveal too much of myself.
I've let people in.
I've gotten to know the human more.
For multiple perspectives.
They are all individually so magical.
And I am a lot cooler than I thought I was.

I waited 30 years until I really started
believing in myself in a way that made me uncomfortable.
I highly recommend you don't wait as long.
The thing about belief is you don't have to wait for it.
You can just, decide to believe.
And all of it's powers just come with it.

One of the first times you felt like you were becoming more you.
Going on that first denver trip by yourself.
Going ziplining by yourself.
Getting over an hour long uber ride.
Making friends with the driver.
Being yourself.
Feeling independent.
That feeling of letting go over the forest of trees into the rockies.
Awkwardly pushing off and giggling with a facial expression of a mischievous kid.
This was freedom.
This was bliss.
This was me.

He started to catch on that I needed someone to believe in me more.
So he started to.
And I felt it.

I can't explain entirely how I feel about you.

But it's different than anything I've ever experienced.

And I've experienced a lot of love, all different kinds.

Something about you.

I feel thrilled.

Always excited.

On my toes but in a good way.

I don't feel the need to ever explain myself to you or with you.

I don't feel like this love will try to put me in a box.

Why are you so different?

So perfect for me?

You make my heart happy.

You make my face smile.

And you bring my racing mind to peace.

I love you.

And I never thought I would.

I never saw this coming.

Not 15 years ago.

Not 5 years ago.

Not 3 months ago.

You.

Are.

It.

Please never change.

Please always be you.

Please always love me.

But if you do have to stop loving me, please never not be you.

You are special.

Not just to me.

But to this world.

I've never met such a rare and perfect soul.

At least not in this life.

You are awe-inspiring.

My soul has latched onto you too much by now.

I don't think I'm going anywhere.

Please just keep being you and I'll stay.

Not that there's a chance I'd leave.

But you make me want to stay here.

If I could make a person for myself with my own hands, I think he'd look like you. And he would definitely act like you.

He would be you.

Maybe I made you in a previous life and asked you to meet me here.

Whatever it is...

Thank you for meeting me.

I'm sorry if I don't remember details about you.
Like if you prefer chocolate to vanilla.
Or coffee to tea.
I'm sorry if I can't remember what your favorite croissant is.
Or where your favorite vacation was.
I may even forget your age...for age is only a number.
I will however remember the way you made me feel.
The way your laugh lines crease when I say something witty.
I'll compartmentalize and sort and place you with the good things.
You will be noted as a pro on my internal pros and cons list for continuing this life.
I will take inventory on a bad day and know that I can call you for a smile.
I may not remember details like your favorite color or favorite number.
But my soul will remember you are a safe place.
A nice place.
And I would rather remember the feeling than what your favorite object is.

Something about writing and having your work put into the world.

Because it's a piece of you now, and a piece of your mind, your soul, that has entered the world in a way you never have before.

And in a way you never could on your own as a being.

With your words and your work, you can touch so many more people than if you go out door to door.

There's something freeing, liberating, soul fulfilling about it.

It should be different. We should all be born into the world on an even keel, at the same level.

Everyone is successful and is respected because we're all on the same level.

We're all millionaires who pursued our passions and made money off of it.

Not from competing or fighting for it.

We didn't hold only a few up on a pedestal for their accomplishments.

For we were all highly accomplished.

There are no "celebrities" or "1%".

We're all allowed to be here and be successful and live our lives the way we damn well choose.

Maybe if we stopped putting others on a pedestal we would see the greatness within ourselves and all the little local businesses around us.

We would encourage our friends more to strive for greatness.

We would encourage ourselves more.

Celebrities are only celebrities because of their fans.

Because people become obsessed with that person and what they are doing.

Even though you could be doing it just as well.

The difference is, you're not.

And you're creating the separation.

Then the media offers support and only shines light on those in this sea of greatness.

It's just like popular kids.

They are only popular because of how other people treat them.

Maybe if you opened up and were your most authentic self and owned that shit then;

a.) you could feel great too

b.) you wouldn't even give a fuck about if people liked you or not.

It doesn't have to be this way.

I'd like to thank all of the people who have been there for me.
Not just this week but in general.
Specifically the last couple years.
These have been some of the biggest years of my life and it's been needed that I have friends.
Those who I can love and rely on if needed.
To have your support.
Your encouragement.
Your love.
The feelings.
To those who have made me feel like Detroit could be a home for me.
And it has been.
You didn't have to love or accept me.
But you did both simultaneously.
To those who made me feel safe.
With all the things that go on in my head and all the things that come out of my mouth.
I appreciate you all.
There aren't many of you.
But the few I have are oh, so important.
The ones you can call at any time if you need them.
And they will truly be there.
No shame, no awkwardness, no judgement.
You are the meaning behind the term "good people"
My people.
Thank you for letting me collect you.
And keep you in my pocket.
For at any moment, when I may need to, I can feel safety in the connection we have made
and you will be there.

I think we're all looking for someone to trust.
Someone to confide in.
That we can tell our demons to and they'll still accept us.
Someone we can ugly cry to and they'll think we're still a badass bitch goddess.
I think we're all looking for someone who accepts us.
Takes us as we are.
Takes us better than we take ourselves.
Shows us parts of ourselves we didn't know existed.
Letting us show every part without judgement.
I think we are all looking for someone that feels a little bit like home.
Or, if you didn't like your home, feels better than home.
Makes you feel like what a home should feel like.
A place to go to where it'll seemingly solve all of your problems right in that moment.
And make you feel better after they go.
A place you can call home.
A person.
They make you better and accept you at your worst.
They make you accept yourself better when you are at your worst.
They prove to you over time that you are better than you say.
You start to believe them because you trust them.
Because they feel like home.
And you begin to trust yourself.
A bond.
To support one another.
To be able to rely on.
A true friendship.
Companionship.
Save-me-ship.
To be there for one another.
To be your most authentic self with.
I think we are all looking for someone like that to go through this crazy scary beautiful adventure with.

The sky looked like an Easter egg you painted with two colors,
how they'd mesh into each other like that.

Of purples and pinks.

I was 33 years old when I realized the amount of barbie dolls I had was in direct proportion to how lonely I was as a child.

I didn't have many friends throughout my youth.

Growing up I was best friends with my mom and dad.

I remember most Fridays as my sisters were growing up and going out to clubs,

I was excited to go to the store where I could pick out a barbie within my parents price range, and potentially an outfit or accessories to go with.

And we would go home and watch a movie on TBS or some other cable movie network.

I would dress my barbie and have her play in barbie world with my other lonely barbies.

I would be thrilled through every moment of watching the movie with my best friends and playing with my new toy.

Looking back, I'm not sure how many barbies I ever had.

But I know I watched a lot of movies with my parents.

I have barbies in my storage unit at my apartment complex.

I have some in storage in a friend's basement.

I've given some away to special little girls in my life who seem to have more friends that I did.

Bitches.

And then there's halloween barbie.

But she's not the point.

To fill a void with all the options of what you could become one day seen in the eyes of a plastic doll who enjoyed The Mummy just as much as you did.

Even holiday barbie had to come out of the box.

What do you mean you keep yours in the box?

Mine had to come out.

Who else was I going to play with?

Oh you have friends?

Well I have barbies and toys and a playhouse and two older best friends who buy my barbies for me.

It's the lonely ones who open the holiday barbie boxes.

We have tons of toys and barbies.

We grow up listening to music in our rooms and making mix tapes.

We learned dances in our rooms without recording it before it was trending.

We learned the lyrics to all our favorite songs.

We would write.

Oh, would we write.

And we would feel.

And we would grow up to learn that that was some of the best things for us in order to navigate this world.

Oh, how you lucked out.

At some point, something feels like an obligation.

Lack of freedom.

Even if you're not doing anything wrong, not conforming to a pattern is viewed as disloyal.

Hurting people.

You can't have friends of the opposite sex. Even if you don't have any friends of the same sex.

You can't do too much on your own.

Obtainment.

Possessive.

You don't get to make your own decisions. Must consider others at all times.

Exhausting.

It feels like a burden to just ask

Feels like a chore, feels like a task

To come drive in through the city,

Pay to park, pay for gas.

It's the second apartment I ever had,

You think they'd be stoked, yea they be glad.

The why's are important because you can sit there and make lists all day but for gratitude we need to know why.

I'm grateful for my warm bed.

But why?

Because it's warm.

But why.

Because it's comfortable.

But why?

Because it's locked inside of my safe home. Because it's a real bed. Because I've never ever bought my own bed until this one. Because I was sleeping on half of a day bed the size of my body and an air mattress before this one. Because it took forever to get delivered. Because it's my bed. It symbolizes independence, freedom, safety, and comfort.

I'm grateful for my warm bed.

We need to know why.

I can barely even bear with the grief.

I wear a broken heart on my sleeve.

Ask me just once and I'll tell you it was fun,

But don't ask me about it again, please.

Take one before you leave.

But don't take no more from me.

I expected the worst which is always a curse;

An interruption in progress and peace.

They say you should always believe,

And that if you don't you'll never be what you'd be,

You can't wait for the courage or the release of a burden

To begin to see what they see.

A smile is what is perceived,

When you hide things just to appease.

At the end of the day, it's all just a game,

And you can't keep taking one for the team.

And we don't always have to agree,

For you are you and I am me,

Part of the beauty of being a human

Is that we view things differently.

Life isn't meant to be free,

It takes work to live out your dreams,

And when you start losing hope and think it's coming to a close,

Remember everything isn't as it seems.

Well fuck it now I guess that's the tea,

And if it is then you didn't hear it from me.

Manifestation from my anxiety blanket,

Aligning my frequency.

I think I was enjoying my time so much I stopped feeling pain.

I'm not sure if I've ever been truly in love at this point. Or if I'm just an adult who seeks and thrives off of excitement. Who has an attention span where if you entertain that excitement long enough, I will stay. I will be attained for that moment in time no matter how long. As long as my excitement is at it's peak and my attention span is not. I don't know if I've ever been truly in love, at this point. Has my ADHD played a trick on me different from any organization trick I've ever seen? If I haven't loved, then why did it feel like it? The excitement attached to our hearts linked us to each other but only until the thrill has stopped. After that, we find new things to get excited about. New things we think we love. Is it excitement? Is it real? How do I know?

I'll let you know when the excitement runs out.

You may have heard the term, beauty is pain. A lot of pretty girls say it. I never agreed with it. It always kind of made me cringe to hear it.

Beauty is pain

I mean, pain often brings out beauty. We see it in paintings, poetry, movies, relationships. But beauty, I think that beauty is just, well, beautiful. There's nothing beautiful about covering up your real face with makeup to create a slightly more tan, cheeky, contoured version of yourself. There's nothing beautiful about having a dotted line drawn on your face so you can feel a percentage closer to your idea of perfect after the procedure. I think all of my friends and family and the women I know look better without makeup, without the botox or the fillers, without the extensions or the "trendy" outfits that you might not even wear if a celebrity you didn't know didn't wear it first. When I can see their natural laugh lines that I know were made from laughing so hard that one time we made skits in our living room. I know it's not up to me and my perception. Everyone can do whatever they want with their own body. Everyone perceives themselves differently. And that's fine. But, don't tell me beauty is pain when beauty is bliss.

Insecurities are pain.

Realizing you're adding an extra layer of makeup, more lashes, more eyeliner, bigger lips, has to look like the picture, has to look like what's-her-name. The makeup isn't enough, I need my face to look permanently perfect in my eyes. Need to be the most looked at girl in the room. Need to be the most fuckable.

That doesn't sound beautiful to me.

I only wish more people did inner work before they made such big changes. Or before they decide spending a car payment on makeup would make them feel better.

I surrender to success and know that I have more control over creating something that may touch someone than making a million dollars. I might as well do the more soul fulfilling, creative pursuit

Making a million dollars is more out of my control than it is to release my art and experiences into the world, which frees my soul so much more than chasing a grind or focusing solely on the numbers. To create. To create anything. But to create art from my experiences. From my brain. From my emotions. From who /am. That connection with whoever it touches. Whoever is moved by what I put out there as a part of me. That will be more fulfilling to me when I die than if I had a yacht with the front end extended so I can land my chopper on it.

It's scary to think I'm capable of so much.

Today marks the 2 year anniversary of me deciding to stay alive.

To live my life intentionally and not just let life take me where it blows me.

I feel like this is what people who find Jesus feel like.

I found the universe.

I found myself.

And it's crazy to say that because I wasn't going to let myself get that far.

Some of you who have known me over 2 years may have noticed some changes. Think I'm nicer. More compassionate. More outgoing. Or maybe the boundaries.

Those of you who met me in the past 2 years probably didn't realize they were meeting me in the midst of such an intense healing period. And I'm grateful for every single amazing soul I've had the privilege of meeting on this healing journey.

I didn't care too much about celebrating birthdays before. Now I really am celebrating my life and making it another year. To be thankful for making it through.

How lucky am I to get to experience this amazing universe with beautiful humans.

Sometimes my love feels like a glove box that won't close.

Just falling out on the ride.

I want to travel the world,

See all that there is to see.

Climb on every mountain,

Swing from every tree.

Paddleboard every lake,

And love turtles in every sea.

Explore every forest,

Step on every crunchy leaf.

Skydive over every deep blue ocean,

And make friends with every cheek.

Never looking back and wondering.

I think this life was made for me.

I want to explore the wild,

Make love to every breeze,

Bend my mind in nature,

Feel a little more like me.

Talk to some animals,

As if they understand me,

Frolic through the flowers,

Just to feel a little more like free.

Drink from melted glaciers,

Take pictures saying "cheese",

Look back and express my gratitude,

Just before I leave.

I want to see the world,

Be all that there is to be,

And if my soul were a painting,

It'd be a Thomas Kinkade scene.

I want to see it all,

And I think it wants to see me too.

Don't you want to see it all?

You just have to choose.

There are people out there waiting to read something you wrote.

Your books

To learn from you and your experiences.

Write for you.

Write for them.

Do you think flowers know how beautiful they'll get?

How big they'll get?

How much space they'll take up?

How lovely they'll smell?

How colorful they'll be?

The joy they can bring people?

Do you think flowers know that they'll grow into something so wondrous?

I know it's not up to them.

It's the environment they're put in.

The people who love them that water them.

That make them flourish.

But, if it were up to them, to the flowers, if they didn't know how big and beautiful and wondrous they could get, do you think that they'd stop growing themselves?

And, if they did, do you think the people watering them would be enough for them to continue to take up space?

I guess my point is, none of us know how great we can become.

And, if we don't, sometimes we stop growing.

But, if we're put in the right environment, with the right people, the people who love us and water us and want us to grow and flourish, I think we'll find that we can continue to grow bigger than we ever imagined.

Because we have to continue to grow even if we don't see how big and wondrous we can become.

We all need encouragement.

Humans and flowers alike.

And now your traditions are my traditions.

All of my hoodie sleeves are made out of tears.
That come from the crevices of 30-year-old fears.

A gentleman so caring,
Kind and sweet,
Sexy and daring,
The chance I'd get to meet.

Talented and witty,
He always makes me laugh,
And I love it when he kisses me,
So I kiss him right back.

Amazingly skilled,
A unique sense of style,
And when he's not making me laugh,
He's making me smile.

Wrapped in his arms,
The comfort I feel,
The safety it brings,
As we both heal.

A warm, gentle soul,
His sensitive side,
The most thoughtful words,
And he wants to be mine?

The way he makes me feel,
So special inside,
Unique and inspirational,
Like I'm worth the while.

His smirk, his voice,
A silver chain necklace,
That smile, those eyes,
A reason to save my messages.
Immediately interested,
There was nothing he lacked
And now when he misses me,
I miss him right back.

His openness and willingness,
His patience with me,
I just hope one day,
He can see what I see.

We're driving up hall road, listening to The City by Hollywood Undead. It's one of the best memories I hold. The feeling. That feeling.

What if he was put into my life at this specific moment, because I asked for it for when I was ready. In my brain, heart, everywhere, I don't feel ready. But, I've never known everything that was best for me. Some of the best things in my life I wasn't ready for. If you don't give it a chance, how do you know if you were ever really not ready for it? Maybe the universe has seen everything I've been doing. It knows I'm ready. It's saying, "she's ready".

Is he a reward for my hardships?
Exactly the man I've always wanted.
Am I a reward for his?

The roses are dead
My favorite color is you
A few weeks and some days
And I'm falling too.

But what if he didn't dance?

And he hated love letters.

What if he made all the wrong things in the kitchen?

And never knew when to ask if you were ok or not?

What if he didn't text you back immediately?

And always ate all of the fries.

What if he didn't love to travel and he hated puppies and didn't like the city and never wanted to go hiking?

...

...

...

But what if he loved you?

And what if he tried?

...

What if he loved watching you dance?

And what if his love letter is making you your favorite cup of coffee in the morning?

What if even though it doesn't turn out just right, the wrong in the kitchen was the right attempt.

And what if he asks when you're ok at the wrong times or not at all but in his mind he's hoping it every second.

And he wouldn't text back immediately but when he does it makes you feel something in your chest and stomach.

He would order an extra side of fries for you.

He would take you on trips even if his passion isn't there as long as you're next to him.

He would love every time you point out how cute a puppy is because you look cute doing it.

He would tolerate the city for the joy it brings to you and on a random Tuesday afternoon he would give you a new pair of hiking shoes because he knows how much adventure lights up your eyes.

And he would love your eyes.

...

What if he doesn't look like the man you had always dreamed of?

What if he doesn't check off every box or contain all the attributes you once thought you needed in a lover?

What if he doesn't know how to dance?

Would you still be able to love him then?

Lanna is a badass
Short and stout
Lives with intention
Is what she's about

Thriving in adventure
Loves to help and mentor
Always brings a hoodie
No matter the type of weather

Commitment and bravery
Some themes that actually saved me
Angel numbers shouting,
"This isn't the way, please!"

Decisions and love
Her biggest enemies she'd hug
Strength and discipline to reach the arrow
When she taught herself self-love

A passion to live
And set herself free
Here to talk about it
because the path that it paved me

New York or California
The airbnbs she'll roam
Wherever she wanders
She'll call herself home.

To those of my loved ones experiencing loss right now.
There is nothing I can say for the pain you are and will continue to feel.
There is nothing I can say to replace the emptiness you feel.
I know from experience that time truly does heal.
So we need patience while we wait for time to pass.
And we need to have grace with ourselves and others while we're patient with the healing and the time passing.

I can however tell you that the pain you feel is a reflection of the amount you loved that particular soul.
The pain you feel is proof of the love you held for them.
It is proof that they were worthy of your love.
And that you were capable of caring for another being so much.
On the days you may not love yourself enough or at all, remember the love you give so freely to others and the space you can hold for the people you love.
The pain you feel right now is only so painful because of how much you were able to love another soul.
Missing another being is perhaps one of the truest ways we learn how we really feel about them.
And we are all so lucky to have something that makes saying goodbye so hard.

Again,
none of this is a good thing.

But I will always try to help.

And I will always try to make art with the broken pieces.

When do you think you'll feel ready to do the thing?

The thing that you wait to do until you feel ready to do it.

Do you think you'll wait all morning?

Maybe you'll be ready in a few days.

Or when you turn 63.

Maybe you'll feel ready once you've already left it here.

Or maybe you'll feel ready 30 years into the next life.

Will you even want to do the thing you want to do anymore by the time you feel ready to do it?

We'll just wait a little longer.

In hopes the feeling arrives.

And we move forward in our life.

This is about recognition.

About recognizing when chapters have closed and it's time to move on.

When your heart is ready to move forward but other parts of you are not.

We weigh down our own journeys by thinking we have control of time. Of what our heart desires. We put forth the "supposed to's" and "should haves" instead of going with the flow and letting life take us on this whirlwind, adrenaline filled, blissful journey of what-could-be's if we let ourselves go.

To be, free.

I imagine a girl out there somewhere in the future who admires me.

She researches me.

What I accomplished while I was here.

What I was well known for.

She reads my books and poetry and tries to understand where I came from.

She resonates with me and my words and tries to learn how I could write from such pain.

"What did she go through?", she will wonder.

More research as she tries to pull in motivation to herself to finish her own books.

Her own dreams.

To conquer her own self-doubt by reading of another's who "made it".

Wondering if she will ever be as well-known as me.

Wondering if her words will ever touch as many people as mine have.

I wonder if there will ever be a girl out there who seeks to understand me the way I seek to understand Sylvia Plath or Virginia Woolf.

You shouldn't wish to be somebody who killed themselves.

Someone who felt and endured so much pain in their life that they felt the need to leave in the middle of a Monday afternoon.

Or a Friday afternoon for that matter.

I imagine a girl out there in need of a friend who turns to books and poetry and the words of others when she needs to feel less alone.

I imagine she finds my words one day and they make her feel something.

She thinks of how we would be friends and have so much in common and so much to talk about.

The way I feel Sylvia Plath and I would hang out and get along so swell.

She would mourn the fact that we weren't born in the same time to embrace each other's company and beautiful, unique minds.

We wouldn't bask in each other's authenticity, only one-sided through years later.

There is a girl out there.

She will find my words through time and read me and resonate.

She will feel empowered in knowing words and personalities can live on.

Her words and personality will live on.

She will learn that other people who she has never met have been through all too similar situations.

She will feel the pain reading my words that I felt while writing them.

And in that moment, she will feel less alone.

And it will matter to her.

And she will go on to pursue her own dreams, that will one day inspire someone else.

She will imagine a girl out there somewhere in the future who admires her.

Who researches her and what she accomplished while she was here and what she was known for.

And she will feel the pain.

And she will feel less alone.

And it will matter.